Baseball: Hall of Fame

Stories of Champions

by SAM and BERYL EPSTEIN

SCHOLASTIC BOOK SERVICES

Published by Scholastic Book Services, a division
of Scholastic Magazines, Inc., New York, N. Y.

BASEBALL: HALL OF FAME, STORIES OF CHAMPIONS is one of the books in the Garrard Sports Library published by Garrard Publishing Company, Champaign, Illinois. Other sports books available in library bindings are:

THE GAME OF BASEBALL
ON THE MOUND
YEA COACH!

2nd printing .... April 1966

Printed in the U.S.A.

Sports Consultant:
COLONEL RED REEDER
Special Assistant to the Director of Athletics
United States Military Academy
West Point, New York

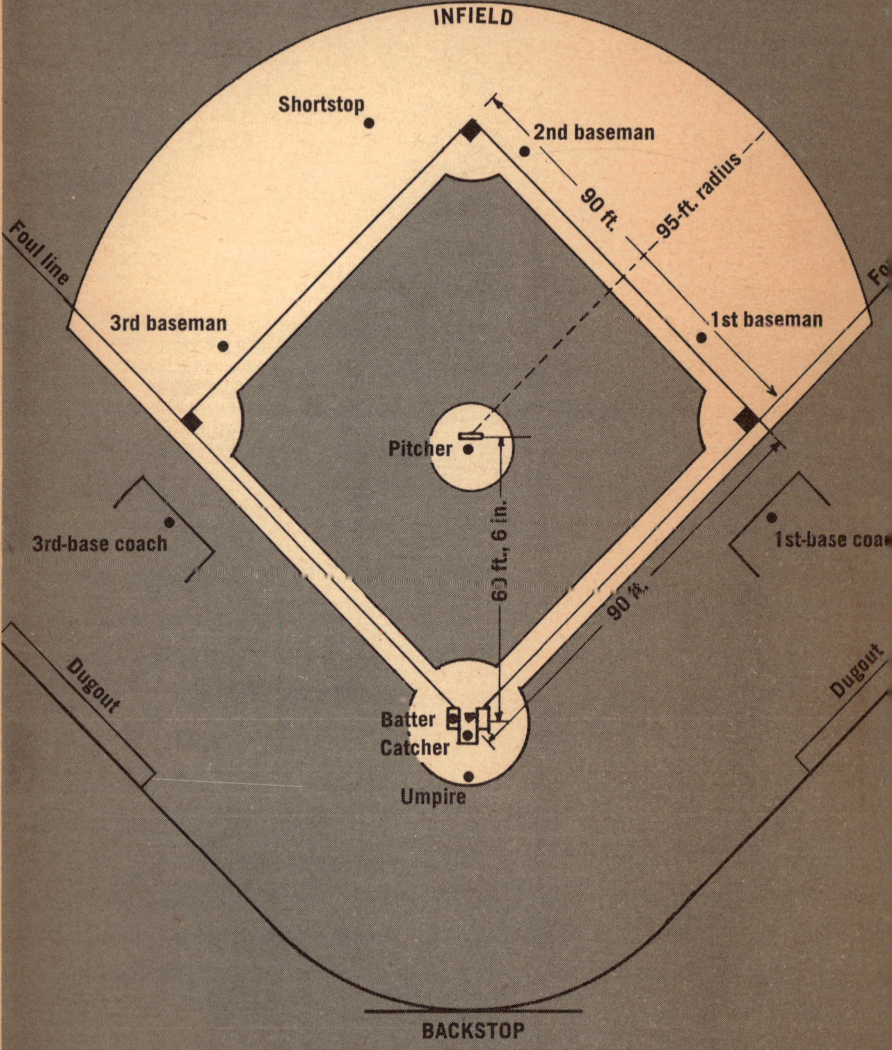
INFIELD
Shortstop
2nd baseman
90 ft.
95-ft. radius
Foul line
3rd baseman
1st baseman
Pitcher
3rd-base coach
60 ft., 6 in.
90 ft.
Dugout
Dugout
Batter
Catcher
Umpire
BACKSTOP

Contents

UNITED PRESS INTERNATIONAL

There is a plaque like Ty Cobb's for everyone in the Baseball Hall of Fame, but not all are famous for their playing. Some have been honored for their part in making baseball the most popular game in America. Some were umpires, or managers, like Connie Mack, who managed the Philadelphia Athletics for 49 years. From the original five, the number of baseball greats in the Hall of Fame has grown to over a hundred — old-timers as well as modern players. (The "moderns," however, must be out of baseball for five years before they can qualify for this highest honor.)

The Baseball Hall of Fame

"Who's going to be named to the Baseball Hall of Fame?"

Thousands of people ask that question each year. Baseball fans answer it with the names of their favorites. Baseball stars hope someday to see their own names on bronze plaques in the marble Hall of Fame at Cooperstown, New York.

Who were the first "Hall of Fame" players?

The first players to be elected to the Baseball Hall of Fame were named in 1936. The Baseball Writers' Association chose them from among all the players in organized baseball up to that time. From the National League, founded in 1876, they named two players: Honus Wagner and Christy Mathewson. From the American League, founded in 1901, they named three players: Ty Cobb, Walter Johnson, and Babe Ruth.

Visitors to the Hall are usually most interested in the players recently elected. But real fans are interested in the old-timers too.

What's in the Baseball Museum?

In the Baseball Museum, in the same building, visitors can see souvenirs of all their favorites.

"Here's Babe Ruth's uniform!" one visitor exclaims. "The Yankees have retired his number. No one on the team wears Number 3."

"Look at Christy Mathewson's glove!" another points out. "And the last uniform Honus Wagner wore!"

"See this picture of Walter Johnson?" a girl

asks. "He married the daughter of a Congressman, you know, and they had six children."

A Little Leaguer says, "Look at the fur hip pads Ty Cobb wore under his uniform! I guess he needed thick sliding pads when he stole all those bases."

Every player named to the Hall of Fame has his own story. In this book you will find five of them — the stories of the five men who first earned baseball's greatest honor.

Honus Wagner, the Flying Dutchman

It was a cold February afternoon in the year 1896. Several young men stood beside the railroad tracks in a little Pennsylvania town. One was John Peter Wagner. His friends called him Honus, or Hans.

"It's your turn, Honus," somebody said.

Honus picked up a stone in his huge right hand. His arm moved back and then snapped forward. The stone flew through the air.

"Look at that!" a friend said. "What's the use

of having a pitching contest with him? Honus throws twice as far as the rest of us, without even trying!"

A stranger came along the tracks. "I'm looking for Honus Wagner," he said.

"That's me," Honus said.

The stranger looked at the tall, awkward fellow. Honus was bowlegged. His arms were so long that his hands seemed to touch his knees. His clothes were shabby, and there was a chicken feather stuck in his derby hat. He looked like a clown.

The stranger laughed.

Honus didn't mind. He just grinned.

"A man in Pittsburgh told me you play ball," the stranger said.

"Sometimes," Honus said. "I used to play on Sundays with my brothers. The rest of the week we all worked in the coal mines."

He picked up a stone as he spoke, and let it fly down the tracks. The stranger could hardly believe his eyes when he saw how far it went.

"Honus isn't telling you the whole story," another young man said. "The Wagner brothers had their own team. It beat all the other teams around here. Al, Honus' brother, is a real professional now. He got Honus a job with an Ohio team last summer."

"What position did you play?" the stranger asked.

Honus looked surprised. "All positions," he said. "I even pitched once in a while."

"What do you do now?" the stranger asked.

"Oh, odd jobs," Honus said. He threw another stone.

Again the stranger watched it fly down the tracks. "My name is Ed Barrow," he said. "I'm signing up players for my team in Paterson, New Jersey. I'm paying the rest of the team $100 a month. But I'll pay you $125. How about it?"

Honus grinned. "That's a lot of money!" he said. "Sure, Mr. Barrow. I'll play for you."

Years later, when Barrow was managing the Yankees, he often told how he had discovered the great Honus Wagner.

"Wagner is the greatest all-round ballplayer of all time," Barrow always said. Many experts agreed with him.

Honus Wagner became the star of the minor-league Paterson team almost overnight. The fans loved him because he was so good-natured. They loved him because he helped the team win games too. He could play well in any position.

"He walks like a crab, fields like an octopus, and hits like the devil!" one sportswriter said.

There was only one major league in those days: the National League. Scouts from almost every National League team came to Paterson to watch the big 22-year-old rookie. Several wanted to buy his contract. Barrow knew Honus was too good to stay in Paterson very long. He sold Honus to Louisville in 1897.

The Louisville manager, Fred Clarke, put Honus in a game against the Baltimore Orioles. This was baseball's roughest team. The Orioles were expert rule breakers. They pulled any trick to win, no matter if it hurt the other players. Honus had never played that way. When he went up to bat, he didn't know what to expect.

He connected with a pitch. It looked like a sure three-bagger. Honus took off like a streak.

The Baltimore first baseman shoved a hip in his way and sent him staggering.

Honus managed to stay on his feet. When he saw the ball still flying toward the outfield, he kept going.

The Oriole second baseman blocked his path. Honus had to run wide around him.

By this time the third baseman had the ball. He tagged Honus so hard he knocked him down.

Manager Clarke yelled at Honus. "You're in the big league now! You can't let anyone push you around like that!"

"All right," Honus said.

Two innings later he sent another line drive into the outfield. The first baseman was ready to shove him aside again. Honus bumped into him at full speed. The Oriole baseman sailed ten feet through the air before he landed.

Honus headed for second without slowing up. The second baseman had seen what happened. He jumped out of the way.

Honus reached third and crashed into the baseman there. He knocked the man flat into the dust.

Then, sitting safely on the base, Honus grinned up at Clarke.

The manager grinned back. "That's the way to play!" he said.

The news spread from team to team. "Don't play rough with Honus Wagner. You'll be sorry if you do!"

BROWN BROTHERS

Honus slides into home in a cloud of dust. Although he was big and awkward, he was a fine base runner.

Honus was glad when other players stopped trying to push him around. He knew he could defend himself if he had to. But he didn't like to fight, on or off the field. He wanted to be friends with everybody.

Ballplayers had a hard life in those days, especially when they were on the road. They stayed in cheap hotels. They changed clothes in bare little shacks. After a game they often had to run for a train. They dried their sweat-soaked uniforms by hanging them out the train windows.

Many players complained. Honus didn't. He cheered up the others by telling them funny stories or playing jokes on his friends. And he didn't mind when they played jokes on him.

Once a friend said, "Would you like to go fishing tonight in my private lake?"

"Sure," Honus said.

That night the friend took him to a lake. The sky was so dark Honus could not see where he was. But he cast in his line and soon he pulled up a fish.

Suddenly some men in police uniforms appeared. They said Honus was fishing in the lake of the city park, and that it was against the law to do that. They took him before a judge.

"Pay a $100 fine and go to jail for 30 days!" the judge said.

"But I have to play ball tomorrow!" Honus said.

Then everyone began to laugh, even the judge.

"It's all right, Honus," the judge said. "We were playing a trick on you. Of course you can play tomorrow! And you'd better win, too! We'll all be there!"

Honus thought it was a good joke. He laughed too.

Honus played for Louisville until the team was broken up in 1900. Then Clarke became manager of the Pirates. He took Louisville's best players

BROWN BROTHERS

with him to Pittsburgh. Honus was one of them. He was glad to be back in Pennsylvania.

In 1901 the American League was started. The owner of the Pittsburgh Pirates knew that some of the new teams wanted Honus.

"Honus," the Pirates' owner said, "you can name your own salary if you will stay with us."

"Why, you don't have to give me a raise!" Honus told him. "I wouldn't think of leaving you."

Honus Wagner always told young players, "Learn to play every position, the way my brothers and I did. Then when your chance comes, wherever it is, you'll be able to take it."

Honus could not only "walk like a crab" and "field like an octopus," but also "hit like the devil." For eight years, he led the League in batting.

During one year with the Pirates, Honus played in seven positions!

That was one of the four years Honus helped the Pirates win the National League pennant. He also helped them beat Detroit in the 1909 World Series. In the seven games of that Series, Honus hit .333. His dazzling speed let him steal six bases to tie a World Series record.

By then Honus Wagner was the team's regular

shortstop. He zigzagged between second and third like a jack rabbit, making stops that looked impossible. His big hands scooped up pebbles along with the ball. His throws to first base crossed the infield like bullets. Experts say he was the greatest shortstop in major-league history.

Honus also won the National League batting championship eight times. He won the base-stealing championship five times.

Honus Wagner played with the Pirates until 1917. He was 43 years old then, and his powerful legs were slowing up. At the end of the season he retired.

But he missed the world of baseball. When the Pirates asked him to come back as a coach in 1933, Honus put on his old uniform. Again he turned out for spring training and traveled with the team from city to city.

Everywhere he went, the fans crowded around to cheer the Flying Dutchman, as they called him.

The Pirates retired his uniform when he left the team in 1952, three years before he died. They felt nobody else had the right to wear that Number 33, which the great Honus Wagner had worn for so long.

HONUS WAGNER'S RECORD

Born, February 24, 1874, at Carnegie, Pennsylvania. Died, December 6, 1955, at Carnegie, Pennsylvania. Height, 5.11. Weight, 200. Threw and batted right-handed.

Batted .300 or better for 17 years (consecutively). Played 100 or more games for 19 years in succession. Played most games in National League, 2,785; most times at bat; most base hits; most one-base hits, 2,426; most two-base hits; most three-base hits.

Abbreviations in chart: G, games; AB, at bat; R, runs; H, hits; 2B, doubles; 3B, triples; HR, home runs; SB, stolen bases; RBI, runs batted in; BA, batting average.

YEAR	CLUB	G	AB	R	H	2B	3B	HR	RBI	BA
1897	Louisville	61	241	38	83	17	4	2	..	.344
1898	Louisville	148	591	80	180	31	4	10	..	.305
1899	Louisville	144	549	102	197	47	13	7	..	.359
1900	Pittsburgh	134	528	107	201	*45	*22	4	..	*.381
1901	Pittsburgh	141	556	100	196	†39	10	6	..	.353
1902	Pittsburgh	137	538	*105	177	*33	16	3	..	.329
1903	Pittsburgh	129	512	97	182	30	*19	5	..	*.355
1904	Pittsburgh	132	490	97	171	*44	14	4	..	*.349
1905	Pittsburgh	147	548	114	199	22	14	6	..	.363
1906	Pittsburgh	140	516	†103	175	*38	9	2	..	*.339
1907	Pittsburgh	142	515	98	180	*38	14	6	*91	*.350
1908	Pittsburgh	151	568	100	*201	*39	*19	10	*106	*.354
1909	Pittsburgh	137	495	92	168	*39	10	5	*102	*.339
1910	Pittsburgh	150	556	90	†178	34	8	4	84	.320
1911	Pittsburgh	130	473	87	158	23	16	9	108	*.334
1912	Pittsburgh	145	558	91	181	35	20	7	94	.324
1913	Pittsburgh	114	413	51	124	18	4	3	55	.300
1914	Pittsburgh	150	552	60	139	15	9	1	46	.252
1915	Pittsburgh	156	566	68	155	32	17	6	78	.274
1916	Pittsburgh	123	432	45	124	15	9	1	38	.287
1917	Pittsburgh	74	230	15	61	7	1	0	22	.265
Major-league Totals		2,785	10,427	1,740	3,430	651	252	101	..	.329

WORLD SERIES RECORD

YEAR	CLUB	G	AB	R	H	2B	3B	HR	RBI	BA
1903	Pittsburgh	8	27	2	6	1	0	0	4	.222
1909	Pittsburgh	7	24	4	8	2	1	0	5	.333
World Series Totals		15	51	6	14	3	1	0	9	.275

*Denotes league leadership.
†Denotes tie for league leadership.

Christy Mathewson, the Big Six

"Strike!" the umpire called.

The man at bat looked dazed. "I didn't even see the ball!" he said.

"We told you Christy could pitch!" a boy yelled.

Almost all the people in Factoryville, Pennsylvania, were crowded around the town diamond that Saturday morning in 1893. They wanted to see if the town team could find a substitute pitcher for its game that afternoon. The regular pitcher had a sore arm.

There had been talk of calling off the game. Then somebody had suggested Christy Mathewson.

"He's only a kid," the man had said. "I think he's 13. But he has a good arm."

"Sure he has!" some of Christy's friends said. "Christy is great!"

So Christy Mathewson came into town from his father's farm. "Show us what you can do, kid," the captain had said.

Christy was showing them.

One by one he struck out the grown men on the team.

"I never saw such speed and control!" the captain said. "We might even win this afternoon!"

Factoryville did win that day. "How about playing with us regularly from now on?" the captain asked.

The big husky boy grinned. "Thanks, sir," he said. "I'd like to."

Christy didn't stay with the Factoryville team long. Larger towns nearby wanted him for their teams. He earned a few dollars for each game. The money went into his college fund.

At 18, Christy entered Bucknell University. He

did well in his classes from the start. He joined the college band and the college choir. He went out for athletics.

Freshmen could play on varsity teams in those days. The football coach looked at Christy's big shoulders and powerful arms and legs.

"I'd like you to try out for football," he said.

Christy grinned. "Baseball is the game I know," he said. "But I'll try."

He took the pigskin and kicked it. It sailed through the air for more than 50 yards!

"You're on the team right now, Mathewson," the coach said.

That autumn Christy helped Bucknell pile up points against Army and Navy. Later he was named All-American.

When winter came, the basketball coach said, "You must be six foot two, Mathewson. You'll be our team's center."

Then came spring and the baseball season. Nobody was surprised when Christy Mathewson became Bucknell's star pitcher.

That summer he played professional ball for the first time. A scout offered him a job with the Taunton ball club, in Massachusetts.

The other team members were like most professional players of those days. They were real roughnecks. They made fun of the rookie who went to college.

"Go back to school, kid!" they told him.

Christy felt homesick and alone. But he stuck it out. He watched every batter, looking for his weak points. He studied Williams, a Taunton pitcher.

Williams sometimes pitched a freak curve ball. It broke down and away, in the opposite direction from the usual curve.

Williams couldn't control the pitch. Christy discovered it needed an inward snap of the wrist. He practiced for hours by himself.

One man he pitched to said, "That ball just sort of fades away from you!"

His words gave the pitch its name, the fadeaway. Later that same curve came to be called a screwball.

The Norfolk club of the Virginia League signed Christy up for the next summer. John Smith, Norfolk manager, gave Christy his first real chance that season of 1900.

"You're starting today," he said as soon as Christy arrived.

"Yes, sir." Christy could feel his muscles tighten up.

He walked the first three men.

"Get a real pitcher!" the fans yelled.

Smith headed for the mound. Christy held his breath.

But Smith didn't take him out. "You'll be all right, son," he said. "Just loosen up. Take it easy."

Christy drew a deep breath. "I'll try."

He wiped his hands on his pants and brushed his hair from his eyes. He wound up. He let the ball fly.

"Strike!"

Christy knew then that he was going to do all right. He did. He won the game.

He won 20 out of the next 22 games he pitched!

"Pack your bag," Smith said one day in July. "The Giants want you!"

Christy could scarcely believe it. He had made the National League, the big league!

He didn't get much chance to pitch that summer. But the next season the manager said, "You will start for us on opening day against the Brooklyn Dodgers."

Everybody said the Dodgers had the best team in the country. The Giants' team was weak. Christy knew why he had been given the job. So did the other Giants.

"The Dodgers are sure to beat us," they said.

Christy Mathewson winding up for his famous pitch.

UNITED PRESS INTERNATIONAL

"The rookie might as well get the loss on his record."

Christy walked slowly out to the mound. "The Dodgers aren't going to win without a fight," he told himself.

He allowed only one run in the first inning, and one in the second. He was hanging on grimly.

Suddenly the Giants seemed to catch his fighting spirit. They scored three runs in the third.

For the next five innings Christy held the Dodgers scoreless. Then, early in the seventh, the Dodgers got another run. That tied the score. They had only one man out and a player on first.

Christy remembered what his friend Smith had said. "Take it easy," he told himself.

He pitched two strikes. He pitched two balls. "Take it easy!" he said again. He looked at the man on first.

Then he sent his fast ball toward the plate. It was a strike! The catcher whipped the ball to first in time to catch the runner there off base. The inning was over. The score was still tied.

Christy's success gave his team another burst of power. They batted in two more runs.

That was all Christy needed. He held the Dodgers for the rest of the game. The Giants won 5 to 3.

It was a great day for Christy. It was a great day for the Giant fans too. They had found a new hero.

The team couldn't keep up its opening-day pace. The Giants finished the year in seventh place. But Christy struck out 215 men in 336 innings. He pitched five shutouts. One was a no-hit, no-run game.

The fans gave their hero a new name. They called him the Big Six. That was the name of a big fire engine New Yorkers were proud of. They thought it was a good name for Christy too.

"The Big Six sure put out the Dodgers' fire!" they said.

Christy didn't return to college that autumn for his senior year. He had decided to stay with the Giants and to take spring training with the team.

Jane, the girl he was in love with, agreed that it was the right thing to do. Christy and Jane had met in college. They planned to be married soon.

"But you can't marry a ballplayer!" some of Jane's friends said. "They're all roughnecks."

"Christy isn't," Jane said. "Christy is different."

The fans said the same thing. They knew Christy spent his evenings reading or playing checkers. He was quiet and modest, and had a good word for everybody. "He's a real gentleman," they said.

The next year, 1902, the Giants got a new manager. He was scrappy little John McGraw. Many players called McGraw the Little Napoleon, and hated him. Others would do anything for him. To Christy he was always a good friend.

McGraw built up a new team. Christy led it to second place in the League in 1903. He struck out 267 batters and won 30 games.

In 1904 Christy won 33 games and the Giants won the League pennant. Big Six was the hero of the nation.

The Giants won the pennant again the next year. And they met the Philadelphia Athletics in the first official World Series. It was an important event in baseball history.

The crowd roared when Christy came to the mound for the first game. He threw only four pitches to retire the side.

Little John McGraw and Christy Mathewson became good friends.

BROWN BROTHERS

For four innings neither side scored. Then Christy himself came to bat and hit a clean single. He and another Giant got home. The score was 2 to 0.

The first Athletic to bat in the eighth got a two-base hit. McGraw didn't even walk to the mound. He was sure Christy could handle it. He was right. Christy struck out the next two men. The third flied out.

The Giants scored one more run in the ninth, to bring their score to 3. Christy Mathewson had won the first official World Series game with a 3-to-0 shutout!

Chief Bender, an American Indian, pitched twice for the Athletics in the 1905 Series.

BROWN BROTHERS

Chief Bender, the Athletics' fine Indian pitcher, shut out the Giants the next day. Then Christy came back to the mound and won the third game.

"Two shutouts, with only a day's rest between! Nobody but the Big Six could have done it," the fans said.

Another pitcher, called Iron Man Joe McGinnity, handed the Athletics their third shutout on the fourth day of play. If the Giants won the next game, they would take the Series.

"Will Christy pitch? Can he possibly pitch three games in just five days?" All over the country people were asking the same questions.

"How about it, Christy?" McGraw asked.

"I'm not tired," Christy told him. "I'd like to pitch again."

Those who saw that game would never forget it. Chief Bender, who had given the Giants their one defeat, seemed to have perfect control. So did Christy. No one scored for four innings.

The Giants got a run in the fifth.

"Hold them now, Christy!" the fan yelled.

The Giants got another run in the eighth.

But Christy Mathewson didn't let the Athletics score once. He won baseball's first World Series by pitching three shutouts in three games!

Christy's teammates were as excited as the fans. "You won for us!" they cried.

"We won together," Christy told them. "You're a great team."

Christy Mathewson led the Giants to three more

The Giants' ball park, the Polo Grounds, looked like this when Christy played for the team. Fans parked their cars behind the outfield and stood there to watch.

BROWN BROTHERS

CULVER PICTURES

Christy became manager of the Cincinnati Reds.

pennants. Then, when his playing began to slow down, he took to managing. He would have been glad to help his friend McGraw manage the Giants. But McGraw wanted Christy to have his own team. Christy took over the Cincinnati Reds.

Christy always found time to help and encourage younger rookies. The Reds loved him and gave him their best. They were on their way to a pennant when Christy had to leave them. He left his wife and young son too, to serve as a captain in World War I.

His job was to teach soldiers how to use gas masks. During one drill, poisonous gas got into his lungs. He died of tuberculosis, caused by that gas, on October 7, 1925.

The next day a huge World Series crowd stood in silent tribute to the Big Six. Christy Mathewson, people said, was master of them all.

CHRISTY MATHEWSON'S RECORD

Born, August 12, 1880, at Factoryville, Pennsylvania. Died, October 7, 1925, at Saranac Lake, New York. Height, 6.01½. Weight, 195. Threw and batted right-handed.

Established modern league record by winning 37 games, 1908; most consecutive innings no bases on balls, 68 (June 19 to July 18, 1913); had 267 strike-outs (modern league record), 1903; won 30 or more games three consecutive years – 1903, 1904, 1905; pitched no-hit games against St. Louis, July 15, 1901, score 5 to 0, and against Chicago, June 13, 1905, score 1 to 0; also against Hampton, 1 to 0, June 12, 1900. Holds National League record with Grover Cleveland Alexander for most games won , 373; pitched three shutouts in 1905 World Series.

Abbreviations in chart: G, games; IP, innings pitched; W, won; L, lost; Pct, percentage; ShO, shutouts; H, hits allowed; SO, strike-outs; BB, bases on balls; ERA, earned runs average.

YEAR	CLUB	G	IP	W	L	Pct	ShO	H	SO	BB	ERA
1900	New York	22	187	20	2	*.909	4	119	128	27	. . .
1901	New York	6	34	0	3	.000	0	34	15	20	. . .
1902	New York	34	276	14	17	.452	8	241	162	74	. . .
1903	New York	45	367	30	13	.698	3	320	*267	100	. . .
1904	New York	48	368	33	12	.783	4	306	*212	78	. . .
1905	New York	43	339	*31	9	.775	*9	252	*206	64	. . .
1906	New York	38	267	22	12	.647	7	262	128	17	. . .
1907	New York	41	315	*24	12	.667	9	250	*178	53	. . .
1908	New York	*56	391	*37	11	.771	*12	281	*259	42	. . .
1909	New York	37	274	25	6	†.806	8	192	149	36	. . .
1910	New York	38	319	*27	9	.750	2	291	*190	57	. . .
1911	New York	45	307	26	13	.667	5	*303	141	38	. . .
1912	New York	43	†310	23	12	.657	0	311	134	34	2.12
1913	New York	40	306	25	11	.694	5	†291	93	21	*2.06
1914	New York	41	312	24	13	.648	5	314	80	23	3.00
1915	New York	27	186	8	14	.364	1	199	57	20	3.58
1916	N.Y.-Cincinnati	13	74	4	4	.500	1	74	19	8	3.04
Major-league Totals . .		635	4,781	373	188	.665	83	4,203	2,505	837	. . .

WORLD SERIES RECORD

YEAR	CLUB	G	IP	W	L	Pct	ShO	H	SO	BB	ERA
1905	New York	3	27	3	0	1.000	3	14	18	1	0.00
1911	New York	3	27	1	2	.333	0	25	13	2	2.33
1912	New York	3	28⅔	0	2	.000	0	23	10	5	1.57
1913	New York	2	19	1	1	.500	1	14	7	2	0.47
World Series Totals . .		11	101⅔	5	5	.500	4	76	48	10	1.15

*Denotes league leadership.
†Denotes tie for league leadership.

Ty Cobb, the Georgia Peach

At 14, Tyrus Cobb was short and skinny. He weighed about 90 pounds. He wanted to grow up to be important like his handsome father, Professor Cobb. The professor ran a newspaper in Georgia, where Ty was born in 1886. The professor was a state senator too.

"Would you like to go to West Point, Ty?" Professor Cobb asked.

BROWN BROTHERS

"I don't want to be an Army officer," Ty answered.

"Then where do you want to go to college? What do you want to do?"

"I don't know," Ty said. He did know that he wanted to do something well. "I have to be the best," he told himself.

One day Ty got a chance to play baseball with the Royston Reds, his town team. As shortstop, he made some good catches. He hit a clean single his first time at bat.

"I know now what I want to do!" he thought. "I want to play baseball."

Ty needed a glove to play with the Reds. He sold two books out of his father's big library to get the money to pay for it. He didn't think his father would miss them.

But the professor did. To punish Ty, he wouldn't let him play ball for many months.

When Ty was 17, he wrote secretly to every town in the new South Atlantic Baseball League. In each letter he offered to play on the town's team. He got only one answer. It came from the Augusta team. The manager said Ty could try out during spring practice. But he would have to pay his own expenses.

Ty told his father what he had done. He asked for the money he needed.

"I don't want you to be a baseball player, Ty," his father said. "You will throw away your life if you spend it playing ball."

All Ty could say was, "I just have to go to Augusta."

Finally the professor said, "All right, son. Get it out of your system. Then you can come home and go to college." He gave Ty the money he had asked for.

Ty didn't get in a single game during spring practice.

On the opening day of the season, the manager said, "One of our regular players is out today, Cobb. I'll have to put you in center field."

Ty did well and was proud of himself. He did well in the next game too. Then the regular center fielder returned.

"Sorry, Cobb," the manager said. "We can't use you any more."

Ty was stunned. He didn't know what to do.

A friend told him about a job with a semipro team in Alabama. Ty telephoned his father. "I want to take that job," he said.

"I understand, son," the professor said. "You don't

want to come home a failure. Go on to Alabama."

Within a few weeks Ty had the best batting average in the little semipro league. The Augusta team had a new manager by then. The man heard about Ty's record and offered him $125 a month to come back. That was a big salary for a rookie in those days.

"I've made good!" Ty thought, when he returned to Augusta. "Now I won't have to play so hard."

One day he was playing in the outfield. He had a bag of popcorn in his hand. A ball came his way. He didn't want to drop the popcorn. He missed the ball.

That night the manager said, "You could be a good ballplayer, Ty. You might even be a famous one someday. But you'll never amount to anything if you don't try harder." Ty was ashamed of himself.

By late summer he had the best batting average in his league. Suddenly the Detroit Tigers bought his contract.

Ty's triumph was saddened, however, for his father had just been killed in an accident. Professor Cobb would never know that his son had made the major leagues.

Ty drove in the two winning runs in his first

Ty hit safely in his first game for Detroit.

game with the Tigers. The older men on the team decided to put the rookie in his place.

"Get back to the sandlot!" they told him. "This game is for men only!" They broke his bats. They made him eat all his meals alone. Nobody would room with him when they were on the road.

Ty thought they would get tired of their razzing soon. They didn't. Then he got angry.

"If I have to fight," he told himself, "I'll fight!"

He fought with his fists. He lost when he battled

men bigger and older than himself. But he always came back for more.

He fought with umpires and with other players on the field too. He learned to slide into the base feet first. If he knocked the baseman down or slashed him with his spikes, he didn't care. The base paths, Ty said, belonged to the runner.

"Cobb is the toughest man in baseball," other players said. "He will do anything to win a game. But he is also one of the best players in the country."

No player ever wanted to win more than Ty Cobb. He felt angry and ill when his team lost.

Every day Cobb tried to make himself a better player. He didn't think he had much natural ability. So he practiced all the time, to make up for it. He also figured out tricks that would help him win games.

As he slid toward a base, for example, he always watched the infielder's eyes. The infielder, of course, was watching the ball. Cobb could tell from the man's eyes where the ball was coming from. Then he knew which side of the base to hit, to save himself from being tagged.

One day the Tigers were in the ninth inning of a game with the Highlanders, later called the Yankees. The score was tied 0-0. Ty got to first base. The next batter tried a bunt, and Ty got to second. The other team expected him to stop there. He kept going. By watching the ball thrown toward third, he managed to let it hit him. The baseman couldn't catch it. Ty got safely on base. Then he stole home.

The next day the Highlanders expected him to steal bases again. Ty knew it. So he didn't try to steal a base for seven innings. The Highlanders stopped watching him closely. Then Ty took off from first on a bunt and got all the way to third!

Cobb was the greatest of the base runners. He worked long hours teaching himself to slide.

CULVER PICTURES

The third baseman was so angry that he slammed the ball on the ground in a high bounce. Ty started off again as soon as he saw the ball in the air. He got home before the baseman could catch the ball and throw it.

Cobb had worked his favorite trick. He described it this way: "Upset the other team and let them beat themselves."

With tricks like that, Ty Cobb broke all records for base stealing. In 1915 he stole 96 bases, a record that stood for 47 years!

Ty won the 1911 batting championship by upsetting his rival, Shoeless Joe Jackson of the Cleveland Indians. Jackson came from the South too. He and Ty had always been friendly.

At the start of a six-game series between the Tigers and the Indians, Jackson greeted Ty the way he always did.

"How you been, Brother Ty?" Jackson asked, grinning.

Ty didn't answer him. He walked away.

Jackson was puzzled. Again he spoke to Ty. Again Ty walked away.

Jackson was so upset that he didn't bat as well as usual that day.

BROWN BROTHERS

Cobb always held his hands apart on the bat. He believed this helped to control his hitting.

The next day the same thing happened. Jackson was even more upset.

All during the series Ty refused to speak to Jackson. Every day Jackson's batting grew worse.

When the series was over, Ty spoke to Jackson again. "Hello, Joe!" he said.

Jackson didn't know Ty had been pulling one of his tricks. Jackson's batting average that year was .408. Ty's was .420.

Every winter Ty Cobb walked 20 or 30 miles a

day to keep himself in shape. He wore pieces of metal in his shoes to make them heavy. Then when he put his playing shoes on in the spring, they felt so light he ran with extra speed.

Cobb always held his hands at least two inches apart on the bat. When he was a skinny boy, that was the only way he could get enough strength behind his swing. Later he found the grip was just right for punching out singles and doubles and placing hits. When he and Honus Wagner met

Ty Cobb at bat.

CULVER PICTURES

for the first time, in the 1909 World Series, photographers crowded around the two stars.

"Come on, let's get the two batting champs together in the batting box!" the photographers said.

Ty and Honus didn't even hear them at first. They were too busy talking about something they had just discovered: big, awkward Honus and wiry, fast Ty Cobb held their bats in exactly the same way!

Cobb could bat the "dead" ball in use when he started to play. He could bat the lively, bouncy "jack-rabbit" ball used after 1920. No other batter made records with both balls as he did. He was American League batting champion 12 times!

In 1911 Cobb was named the League's most valuable player for the year. He was the first choice of every expert voting. This high honor was paid only to Cobb and to Babe Ruth.

Ty Cobb played with the Tigers from 1905 to 1926. He also managed the team from 1921 to 1926. He was more than 40 years old then. But Connie Mack, one of baseball's smartest managers, knew Cobb was still a valuable player. He hired him to play with the Athletics. That year Cobb stole 22 bases and hit .357 in 134 games.

Altogether Ty Cobb played 3,033 games, more than any other major-league baseball player. His plaque in the Hall of Fame says he "created or equalled more major league records than any other player."

Ty Cobb had won his boyhood ambition. He grew up to be somebody important. His home town, Royston, was proud of the Georgia Peach, as Ty's fans called him. Royston was also proud of the hospital Cobb built there and the fund he set up to help students go to college.

Cobb was able to build that hospital and set up that fund because he had broken one more record. By investing his money wisely, he had become the first millionaire player in baseball.

TY COBB'S RECORD

Born, December 18, 1886, at Narrows, Georgia. Died, July 17, 1961, at Atlanta, Georgia. Height, 6.00¾. Playing weight, 175. Threw right-handed and batted left-handed.

Holds league record for games played, times at bat, runs scored, stolen bases, hits and three-base hits; most times five hits in one game, season, four (1922); six hits in six times at bat, May 5, 1925. Stole 892 bases during major-league career, leading American League six times; stole 96 in 1915 for league record.

YEAR	CLUB	G	AB	R	H	2B	3B	HR	SB	RBI	BA
1905	Detroit	41	150	19	36	6	0	1	2	..	.240
1906	Detroit	97	350	44	112	13	7	1	23	..	.320
1907	Detroit	150	605	97	*212	29	15	5	*49	*116	*.350
1908	Detroit	150	581	88	*188	*36	*20	4	39	*101	*.324
1909	Detroit	156	573	*116	*216	33	10	*9	*76	*115	*.377
1910	Detroit	140	509	*106	196	36	13	8	65	88	*.385
1911	Detroit	146	591	*147	*248	*47	*24	8	*83	*144	*.420
1912	Detroit	140	553	119	*227	30	23	7	61	90	*.410
1913	Detroit	122	428	70	167	18	16	4	52	65	*.390
1914	Detroit	97	345	69	127	22	11	2	35	57	*.368
1915	Detroit	156	563	*144	*208	31	13	3	*96	95	*.369
1916	Detroit	145	542	*113	201	31	10	5	*68	67	.371
1917	Detroit	152	*588	107	*225	*44	*33	7	*55	108	*.383
1918	Detroit	111	421	83	161	19	*14	3	34	64	*.382
1919	Detroit	124	497	92	†191	36	13	1	28	69	*.384
1920	Detroit	112	428	86	143	28	8	2	14	63	.334
1921	Detroit	128	507	124	197	37	16	12	22	101	.389
1922	Detroit	137	526	99	211	42	16	4	9	99	.401
1923	Detroit	145	556	103	189	40	7	6	9	88	.340
1924	Detroit	†155	625	115	211	38	10	4	23	74	.338
1925	Detroit	121	415	97	157	31	12	12	13	102	.378
1926	Detroit	79	233	48	79	18	5	4	9	62	.339
1927	Philadelphia	134	490	104	175	32	7	5	22	93	.357
1928	Philadelphia	95	353	54	114	27	4	1	5	40	.323
Major-league Totals	...	3,033	11,429	2,244	4,191	724	297	118	892	1,901	.367

WORLD SERIES RECORD

YEAR	CLUB	G	AB	R	H	2B	3B	HR	SB	RBI	BA
1907	Detroit	5	20	1	4	0	0	0	0	0	.200
1908	Detroit	5	19	3	7	1	0	0	2	3	.368
1909	Detroit	7	26	3	6	3	0	0	2	5	.231
World Series Totals	......	17	65	7	17	4	1	0	4	8	.262

*Denotes league leadership.
†Denotes tie for league leadership.

Walter Johnson, the Big Train

It was Saturday afternoon in the little town of Weiser, Idaho. Most people were watching their town ball team. The six-footer on the mound had big hands and very long arms. When his right arm whipped forward, the ball streaked over the plate like a bullet.

"What a speedball!" a man in the stands said to the fan next to him. "Who is that pitcher?"

The fan stared. "You must be a stranger!" he said. "That's Walter Johnson, star of our Weiser team."

The stranger was a traveling salesman who loved baseball. He had seen hundreds of games. But he had never seen a pitcher like Walter Johnson.

That night he wrote a letter to Joe Cantillon, manager of the Washington Senators.

"You better come out here and get this pitcher," he wrote. "He throws a ball so fast nobody can see it, and he strikes out everybody. . . . His control is better than Christy Mathewson's. He knows where he's throwing, because if he didn't there would be dead bodies strewn all over Idaho. So you'd better hurry, Joe, or you'll be sorry."

Joe Cantillon couldn't afford to send a scout to Idaho right away. Then Cliff Blankenship, his catcher, broke a finger and couldn't play. Cantillon sent him to Kansas to look at a player he had heard about there.

"Then go to Weiser, Idaho," Cantillon said, "and take a look at a fellow named Walter Johnson."

Blankenship couldn't believe his eyes when he saw Walter pitch.

"How old are you, son?" he asked the young ballplayer after the game.

Walter was shy, meeting a big-league catcher. "Almost 20," he said.

"You must have been throwing a ball ever since you could walk," Blankenship said.

Walter shook his head. "There was no one to play with on the Kansas farm where I was born," he said. "So I never got to play at all until my folks moved to California. I was 14 then. I pitched for my high-school team, and played some semipro ball. And I've been playing semipro ball for Weiser ever since I drifted out here."

"How would you like to pitch for the Washington Senators?" Blankenship asked.

Walter Johnson pitched his first major-league game for the Senators on August 2, 1907. He lost to Detroit 3 to 2. Detroit was the best team in he American League that year. Washington was about the worst.

But Walter surprised Detroit's players that day. The best hitters struck out time after time. Ty Cobb was one of them.

"You can't hit what you can't see," Cobb said.

Five days later Walter pitched against Cleveland. He allowed only four hits. The Senators won 7 to 2. The fans tried to carry Walter off the field after his victory.

Soon newspapers were full of stories that said Walter Johnson could throw a ball faster than anyone else. One sportswriter called him the Big Train. He said Walter's fast balls sped to the plate as fast as an express train.

People said Walter was a real gentleman, like Christy Mathewson. Walter never argued with umpires. He always spoke in a quiet, gentle voice. He didn't brag when he won.

Johnson was one of baseball's best-liked men. He even got along with Ty Cobb (right).

CULVER PICTURES

In those days pitchers often tried to scare batters away from the plate by throwing right at them. Walter never did that on purpose. But he did have trouble, at first, controlling the ball. Some players were afraid to bat against him because his wild pitches were thrown so hard. With practice, Walter learned control.

Most batters said Walter's fast ball was almost impossible to hit. But when the Senators were ahead, he sometimes gave a batter a chance.

"Why did you let that bum hit?" his teammates would ask.

"Shucks!" Walter answered. "He hasn't had a hit in days. Baseball is no fun unless you can hit once in a while."

Walter didn't ease up when his own team was behind, however. Then he used so much power that he grunted each time he threw the ball.

"The Big Train is turning on extra steam today," players said when they heard him grunt. "We're going to have trouble seeing the ball."

In 1913 Walter Johnson pitched 56 scoreless innings from April 10 to May 15. During that winning streak he shut out the Yankees, the Athletics, the White Sox, and the Red Sox!

In that same season he won 36 games and lost

CULVER PICT

While his teammates watch, Walter is given a new car. This was 1913, one of his best years.

only seven. He was the leading American League pitcher that year. He led his League four other years, too.

But not all the Washington Senators were as good as Walter. People made fun of the team. One favorite joke was: "Washington: first in war, first in peace, and last in the American League."

Walter helped the Senators climb up out of the bottom of the League. They even reached second place. But they could never win the pennant.

"It's too bad Walter pitches for the poor old

Senators," people said. "As long as he stays with that team, he'll certainly never get a chance to pitch in a World Series."

But in 1924 the Senators surprised the country. They played like champions and won their first pennant.

"At last!" some people said. "Now the Big Train can beat the Giants in the Series."

Others said, "It's too late! He's 36 years old. His fast ball isn't what it used to be."

The Washington ball park was packed for the first game. President Calvin Coolidge threw out the first ball. Walter was on the mound.

The game lasted 12 innings. Walter struck out 12 Giant batters and set a new record. But the Giants won 4 to 3.

The Senators won the second game. The Giants won the third. Then the Senators won the fourth and tied the Series.

Walter pitched again in the fifth game. The Giants battered him for 13 hits and won 6 to 2. If they won the next game, they would win the Series.

It was a sad day for Washington. It was even sadder for Walter Johnson. He had waited 18 years to pitch in a World Series. And he had lost both games he had pitched.

The Senators made up their minds to win the next game for Walter. They did, with Tom Zachary on the mound. Again the Series was tied. The winner of the next game would be the world champions.

Walter sat on the bench when the game started. For three innings there was no score. The Senators got one run in the fourth. But the Giants scored three times in the sixth.

The Senators didn't give up. In the eighth inning they tied the score.

Then the Wasington manager called on the Big Train. "You're the best we have, Walter," he said. "We're going to win or lose with you."

The fans stood up and cheered when Walter walked out to the mound in the ninth inning. They were telling him they were glad he was going to have another chance.

The Giants got two men on base that inning. But they couldn't score a run.

The Senators didn't score either. The tenth inning was also scoreless. So was the eleventh.

When the twelfth inning started, the sun was setting. The Giants would have extra trouble seeing Walter's fast ball. And he was grunting. He was turning on all the steam he had.

The Giants couldn't score.

Then the Senators came to bat. The first man up was put out at first. The second got a two-base hit. Walter was up next. He got to first on an error.

The next Senator up was Earl McNeely. He hit an easy grounder toward third. The fans groaned.

But the ball took a crazy bounce. It leaped over the third baseman's head. Washington scored a run!

The game was over. The Senators were the world champions. Walter had won his World Series.

The Senators won the American League pennant the next year too. Walter pitched the first World Series game. He beat the Pittsburgh Pirates 4 to 1. He shut them out in the fourth game 4 to 0.

In the seventh game, the deciding game, luck was against him. Rain was falling. The ball was slippery and hard to control. Walter's tiring arm was chilled. He lost 9 to 7, and Pittsburgh won the Series.

Walter Johnson stopped pitching in 1927. He had been with the Senators for 21 seasons. He was 40 years old. After that, he managed several teams, including the Senators. He died in 1946.

Walter Johnson was one of baseball's greatest pitchers. He won 413 of the 802 games he pitched

Johnson managed the Cleveland Indians as well as the Senators and other clubs.

for the Senators, to set a League record. He shut out his opponents 113 times, a record for both leagues.

Walter Johnson was also a real gentleman and a great sportsman.

WALTER JOHNSON'S RECORD

Born, November 6, 1887, at Humboldt, Kansas. Died, December 10, 1946, at Washington, D. C. Height, 6.01. Weight, 200. Threw and batted right-handed.

Pitched most games in American League history, 802; equaled major-league record for pitching most successive complete games played by club, 3 (September 4, 5, and 7, 1908), all shutouts; won most games, league, 416; tied league mark for most consecutive games won, 16 (July 3 to August 23, 1912); holds American League record for most shutout games, 113; pitched most consecutive shutout innings, 56 (April 10–second inning to May 14–fourth inning, 1913); pitched 1-0, no-hit game against Boston American League, July 1, 1920.

YEAR	CLUB	G	IP	W	L	Pct	ShO	H	SO	BB	ERA
1907	Washington	14	111	5	9	.357	2	100	70	16	...
1908	Washington	36	257	14	14	.500	6	196	160	52	...
1909	Washington	40	297	13	25	.342	4	247	164	84	...
1910	Washington	†45	*374	25	17	.595	8	*262	*313	76	...
1911	Washington	40	322	25	13	.658	6	292	207	70	...
1912	Washington	50	368	32	12	.727	7	259	*303	76	...
1913	Washington	48	*346	*36	7	*.837	*12	232	*243	38	*1.14
1914	Washington	*51	*372	*28	18	.609	*10	*287	*225	74	1.72
1915	Washington	47	*337	*27	13	.675	†8	258	*203	56	1.55
1916	Washington	48	*371	*25	20	.556	3	*290	*228	82	1.89
1917	Washington	47	328	23	16	.590	8	259	*188	67	2.28
1918	Washington	39	325	*23	13	.639	†8	241	*162	70	*1.27
1919	Washington	39	290	20	14	.588	*7	235	*147	51	*1.49
1920	Washington	21	144	8	10	.444	4	135	78	27	3.13
1921	Washington	35	264	17	14	.548	1	265	*143	92	3.51
1922	Washington	41	280	15	16	.484	*4	283	105	99	2.99
1923	Washington	42	261	17	12	.586	3	263	*130	69	3.48
1924	Washington	38	278	*23	7	*.767	*6	233	*158	77	*2.72
1925	Washington	30	229	20	7	.741	3	211	108	78	3.07
1926	Washington	33	262	15	16	.484	2	259	125	73	3.61
1927	Washington	18	108	5	6	.455	1	113	48	26	5.08
Major-league Totals		802	5,924	416	279	.599	113	4,920	3,508	1,353	...

WORLD SERIES RECORD

YEAR	CLUB	G	IP	W	L	Pct	ShO	H	SO	BB	ERA
1924	Washington	3	24	1	2	.333	0	30	20	11	3.38
1925	Washington	3	26	2	1	.667	1	26	15	4	2.08
World Series Totals		6	50	3	3	.500	1	56	35	15	2.70

*Denotes league leadership.
†Denotes tie for league leadership.

Babe Ruth, Sultan of Swat

Babe Ruth's real name was George Herman Ruth, but nobody called him that. Newspaper reporters called him the Home Run King or the Sultan of Swat or the Bambino. Men who played with him called him the Big Guy. His fans called him Babe, or the Babe.

When they saw him on the street they would shout, "Hiya, Babe!" The Babe always answered.

BROWN BROTHERS

He loved everybody, and everybody loved him. He especially loved children.

Once, during a World Series, a doctor asked the Babe to visit a sick boy in a New Jersey hospital.

"He will not even try to get better," the doctor said. "I'm afraid he will die. But you're his hero, Babe. If he could see you, maybe he would try to get well."

The next morning Babe Ruth left New York and drove to New Jersey. In the hospital he sat down beside the boy's bed. He told him baseball stories. He gave him a bat and a ball.

"Listen to your radio this afternoon, Johnny," the Babe said as he left. "I'm going to hit a homer just for you."

That afternoon the Yankees played the St. Louis team. Babe did what he had said he would do: he hit a home run.

The boy began to get better. Soon he was well again. He always said he owed his life to Babe Ruth.

Babe was born in Baltimore, Maryland, in 1895. He was one of five children. His parents were poor and had very little time for him. He ran wild in the streets. When he was seven years old he was put into St. Mary's School. This was a home for orphans and for children, like Babe, who got into trouble.

At St. Mary's he learned to play ball. Soon he was the best player in the school. He could play any position. The school's coach brought the manager of a minor-league Baltimore team to see him. The manager hired Babe immediately.

Babe pitched in his first professional game on April 22, 1914. He was a tall, awkward 19-year-old, with a big body and thin legs. He stood and walked pigeon-toed. He threw left-handed. In that first game he pitched a shutout. He also hit a two-bagger. His team won 6 to 0.

The Boston Red Sox bought Ruth later that season. During the next four years he became a famous pitcher. In two of those years he won 23 games a season. He pitched against the great Walter Johnson in eight games and won six of them. He helped the Red Sox win three pennants.

The Red Sox manager was Ed Barrow, the man who discovered Honus Wagner. Barrow knew he had another great player in Babe Ruth. Then Babe proved he could bat as well as he could pitch. In an exhibition game in 1919, he hit a ball 597 feet. This is over a tenth of a mile!

"You can't keep a batter like that out of the

CULVER PICTURES

Babe Ruth began setting records as a pitcher for the Boston Red Sox.

line-up," Barrow said. "He should be batting every day."

A pitcher does not play every day because he must have rest. So Barrow put Babe in the outfield. That meant Babe could be in the line-up every game.

Other teams wanted to buy Babe Ruth's contract. The Red Sox wanted to keep him. Then the Red Sox owner needed money and sold Babe to the Yankees for $100,000. No club had ever paid that much for a player.

That same year, 1920, Babe Ruth hit 54 home runs!

Before that time, few players really tried to hit the ball out of the park. They played what is called an "inside" game. They tried for singles and doubles. They bunted and made sacrifice plays in order to help their team score.

When the Red Sox made Babe Ruth an outfielder, he became one of Boston's star hitters.

BROWN BROTHERS

But the fans loved to see Babe swat the ball over the fence. He was showing them an exciting new kind of baseball. They jammed the stands whenever he played.

Babe gripped the bat at the end of the handle, his hands close together. (Compare with Ty Cobb's grip, page 47.)

CULVER PICTURES

Other batters began to copy the Babe. They began to "swing from the heels," to try and hit home runs. A new, livelier "jack-rabbit" ball was being used now too. It traveled farther when the bat struck it, and helped pile up homers.

Baseball became a sluggers' game. But the Babe was the mightiest slugger of them all. In 1921 he hit 59 home runs, and the Yankees won the American League pennant for the first time.

Babe Ruth was paid $30,000 that year, a huge salary for those days. It seemed especially big to the Babe, who had been so poor as a boy. He had a good time spending it. He bought a big red car. He smoked big fat cigars. He gave big parties. He ate huge meals.

"This is no way to keep in training, Babe," the team manager said. "You'll get fat and slow!"

The Babe just laughed. "I can take care of myself," he said.

He spent part of the winter playing exhibition games. This was against a strict major-league rule. Babe was in serious trouble.

He was punished for breaking the rule. He was not allowed to join the Yankees until six weeks after the season started. Even then he was not in playing condition because he had not kept in training. His record that year was very poor.

A New York state senator made a speech about the Babe at a baseball writers' dinner. The Babe was there.

"You let our team down, Babe," the senator said. "You let all your fans down. Worst of all,

Babe sometimes got in trouble on the field, too. In a game against Washington he ran into the right-field wall, knocking himself out.

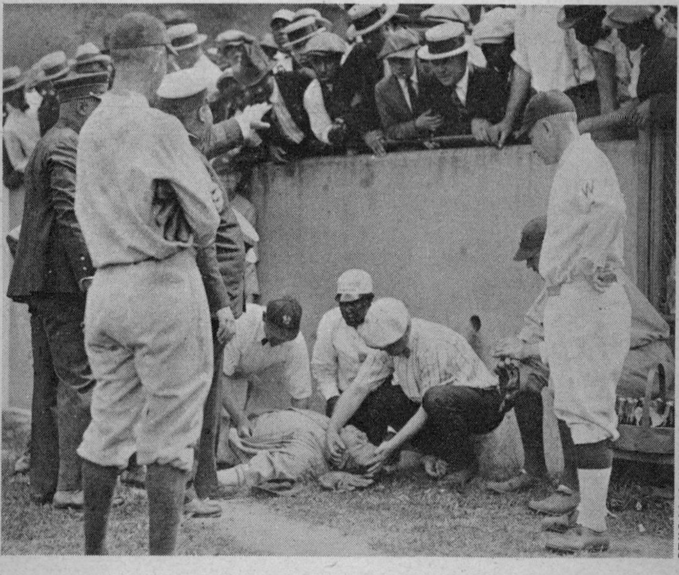

CULVER PICTURES

you disappointed all the boys who look up to you as a hero."

There were tears in the Babe's eyes. "You're right," he said quietly. "From now on I will obey the rules. I'll try never to let people down again."

And he did try. But many times after that he broke rules. Each time he was punished in one way or another. Once he paid a $5,000 fine because he refused to obey the team manager. Once he got sick and could not play for weeks because he ate too many hot dogs.

But when Babe Ruth obeyed the rules, he led his team to the top of the League. His home runs helped the Yankees win the pennant seven times. In 1927 he hit his record of 60 homers.

The Yankees made so much money that in 1923 they built their own stadium. Everybody called the new Yankee Stadium "The House That Ruth Built." On opening day, 70,000 fans jammed the stands to watch the Babe. He gave them a good show. He hit a homer with two men on base. The Yankees won the game 4 to 1.

The Babe always thought he could do anything he wanted. Usually he could. But in 1934 the Babe wanted the Yankees' manager fired. "I don't like

him," he said. The owner of the Yankees refused.

"If he doesn't go, I go!" Babe Ruth threatened.

Still the owner stood firm. And so Babe Ruth left the Yankees.

The Babe joined the Boston Braves the next season. But he was 40 years old. He had been with the majors for 21 years. His great playing days were over. He retired even before the season ended.

He still loved the game. And he still loved children. For the rest of his life he worked to give boys a chance to play baseball. He helped the American Legion organize boys' baseball teams all over the country.

In 1948, Yankee Stadium was 25 years old. Everyone wanted the Babe to attend its big birthday celebration. He was very sick by then. He was soon to die. But he put on his old Number 3 uniform once more and walked slowly out onto the field. Thousands of fans cheered. They wanted him to know that they had not forgotten the mighty Bambino.

Fans have not forgotten the Bambino and his home runs to this day. The home run they most

On September 30, 1927, Babe hit his sixtieth home run of the season. This picture was taken just after he hit the ball.

WIDE WORLD PHOTOS

often talk about happened in the 1932 World Series.

The Yankees were playing the Chicago Cubs. The Yankees had already won two games. When the Babe trotted out on the field for the third game, the Chicago fans booed him. They wanted to upset

Babe Ruth was a hero to boys throughout the country and to thousands of fans all over the world.

WIDE WORLD PHOTOS

him so he would strike out. The Babe laughed.

In the fifth inning the score was tied. Babe had already hit one homer. Now he was coming up to bat again. The Chicago fans booed louder than ever.

The umpire called the first pitch a strike. The Babe grinned and held up a finger. He seemed to be saying, "That's right. It was a strike. So what?"

When the next pitch came over for strike two, the Babe held up two fingers. Now the Chicago fans roared happily.

Then the Babe pointed a finger at a spot in the center-field stands. He seemed to be telling everybody exactly where he was going to hit the next ball.

The pitcher wound up once more. Babe watched him. As always, he was holding his head absolutely still. As always, his bat was over his shoulder. The end of it twitched just a little, like the tail of a cat about to pounce.

The third pitch streaked toward the plate. The Babe swung and hit. The ball soared high into the air. Every fan lifted his head to follow its flight. The ball disappeared, right into the center-field stands!

For a second there was silence. Then everybody in the ball park stood up and cheered.

It was a gigantic homer. The Yankees won the game. They won the Series too.

Later a newspaper man said, "Suppose you'd struck out, Babe, after bragging about where you were going to hit that ball. Wouldn't you have felt foolish?"

The Babe looked surprised. "Gee!" he said. "I never thought of that!"

The Babe was always sure he could do anything he wanted. Sometimes he failed. But not that day in Chicago in 1932. That day he made baseball history.

BABE RUTH'S RECORD

Born, February 6, 1895, at Baltimore, Maryland. Died, August 16, 1948, at New York, New York. Height, 6.02. Weight, 215. Threw and batted left-handed.

Filled record books with home-run and other slugging marks, including most homers for major-league career, 714, and in one season, 60 in 1927; also most runs batted in, majors, 2,209; most bases on balls, majors, 2,056, and season, 170 in 1923.

YEAR	CLUB	G	AB	R	H	2B	3B	HR	RBI	BA
1914	Boston	5	10	1	2	1	0	0	0	.200
1915	Boston	42	92	16	29	10	1	4	20	.315
1916	Boston	67	136	18	37	5	3	3	16	.272
1917	Boston	52	123	14	40	6	3	2	10	.325
1918	Boston	95	317	50	95	26	11	†11	64	.300
1919	Boston	130	432	*103	139	34	12	*29	*112	.322
1920	New York	142	458	*158	172	36	9	*54	*137	.376
1921	New York	152	540	*177	204	44	16	*59	*170	.378
1922	New York	110	406	94	128	24	8	35	96	.375
1923	New York	152	522	*151	205	45	13	*41	†130	.393
1924	New York	153	529	*143	200	39	7	*46	121	*.378
1925	New York	98	359	61	104	12	2	25	66	.290
1926	New York	152	495	*139	184	30	5	*47	*155	.372
1927	New York	151	540	*158	192	29	8	*60	164	.356
1928	New York	154	536	*163	173	29	8	*54	†142	.323
1929	New York	135	499	121	172	26	6	*46	154	.345
1930	New York	145	518	150	186	28	9	*49	153	.359
1931	New York	145	534	149	199	31	2	†46	163	.373
1932	New York	132	457	120	156	13	5	41	137	.341
1933	New York	137	459	97	138	21	3	34	103	.301
1934	New York	125	365	78	105	17	4	22	84	.288
1935	Boston	28	72	13	13	0	0	6	12	.181
Major-league Totals		2,502	8,399	2,174	2,873	506	136	714	2,209	.342

(Continued on next page.)

WORLD SERIES RECORD

YEAR	CLUB	G	AB	R	H	2B	3B	HR	RBI	BA
1915	Boston	1	1	0	0	0	0	0	0	.000
1916	Boston	1	5	0	0	0	0	0	0	.200
1918	Boston	3	5	0	1	0	1	0	2	.200
1921	New York	6	16	3	5	0	0	1	4	.313
1922	New York	5	17	1	2	1	0	0	1	.118
1923	New York	6	19	8	7	1	1	3	3	.368
1926	New York	7	20	6	6	0	0	4	5	.300
1927	New York	4	15	4	6	0	0	2	7	.400
1928	New York	4	16	9	10	3	0	3	4	.625
1932	New York	4	15	6	5	0	0	2	6	.333
World Series Totals	....	41	129	37	42	5	2	15	32	.326

PITCHING RECORD

YEAR	CLUB	G	IP	W	L	Pct	H	BB	SO	ERA
1914	Boston	4	23	2	1	.667	21	7	3	3.91
1915	Boston	32	218	18	8	*.692	166	85	112	2.44
1916	Boston	44	324	23	12	.657	230	118	170	*1.75
1917	Boston	41	326	24	13	.649	244	108	128	2.02
1918	Boston	20	166	13	7	.650	125	49	40	2.22
1919	Boston	17	133	9	5	.643	148	58	30	2.97
1920	New York	1	4	1	0	1.000	3	2	0	4.50
1921	New York	2	9	2	0	1.000	14	9	2	9.00
1930	New York	1	9	1	0	1.000	11	3	2	3.00
1933	New York	1	9	1	0	1.000	12	3	0	5.00
Major-league Totals	......	163	1,221	94	46	.671	974	442	487	2.28

WORLD SERIES PITCHING RECORD

YEAR	CLUB	G	IP	W	L	Pct	H	SO	BB	ERA
1916	Boston	1	14	1	0	1.000	6	3	4	0.64
1918	Boston	2	17	2	0	1.000	13	7	4	1.06
World Series Totals	....	3	31	3	0	1.000	19	10	8	0.87

*Denotes league leadership.
†Denotes tie for league leadership.